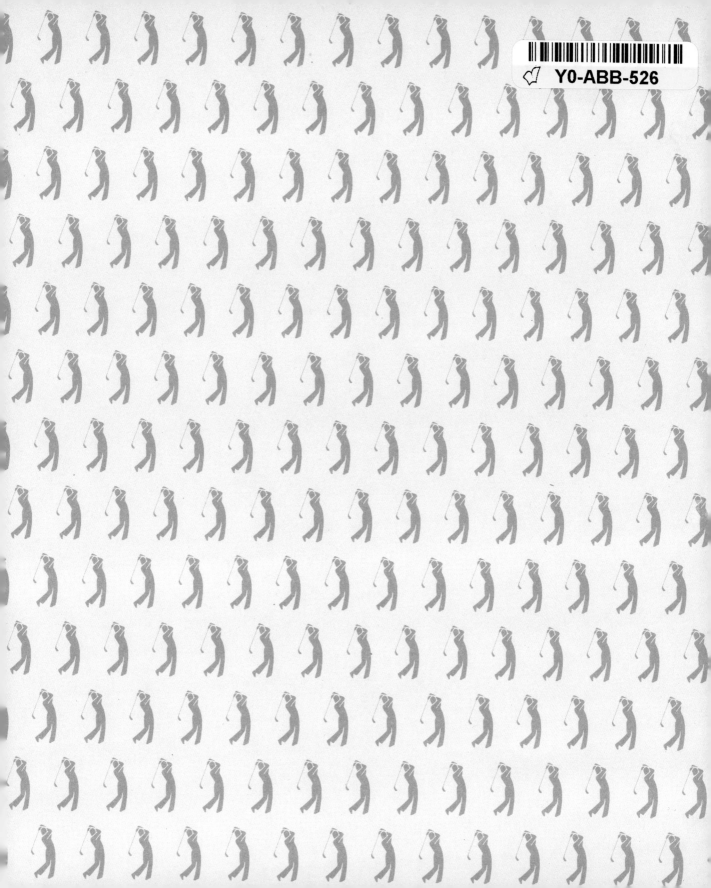

GOLF

ESSENTIALS

STEP-BY-STEP TECHNIQUES TO IMPROVE YOUR SKILLS

GOLF
ESSENTIALS

STEP-BY-STEP TECHNIQUES TO IMPROVE YOUR SKILLS

STEVE NEWELL

LORENZ BOOKS

This edition first published in 1998 by Lorenz Books

Lorenz Books is an imprint of Anness Publishing Limited
Hermes House, 88-89 Blackfriars Road
London SE1 8HA

ISBN 1 85967 700 2

A CIP catalogue record for this book is available from the British Library

Publisher: Joanna Lorenz
Design: Twin
Photographers: David Cannon and Susan Ford

Printed in Hong Kong / China

10 9 8 7 6 5 4 3 2 1

All instructions in this book are provided for right handed players.

CONTENTS

INTRODUCTION

Golf consists of an intricate series of movements, which the player must put together to hit the golf ball with a combination of power and accuracy. As if the odds of swinging a small clubhead more than 6 m (20 ft) up and around your body at speeds of up to 120mph were not daunting enough, the course itself is vast and dotted with cunningly-placed hazards.

It sounds scary, doesn't it? Far from being complicated, however, a great golf swing is based on a set of fairly simple fundamentals, all of which are within anyone's grasp. This is true at any level. Those spectacular shots that professional golfers play all stem from an understanding of golf's basic techniques.

Golf Essentials is an easy-reference manual explaining golf's fundamentals – the building blocks of an efficient golf swing. Whether you have just taken up the game, or have been playing for years and perhaps hit something of a "brick wall" in terms of progress, this book can help you. The sharp photography and clear concise writing enable you to absorb the theories of the golf swing and to put them into practice. The book also tackles the game's most persistent faults, suggests ways to cure them, and there's equipment advice, providing guidance in a market dominated by high-technology and space-age materials.

Golf Essentials takes you back to basics, which is the only way to take a step forward. You can play this game throughout your lifetime, and a sound knowledge of the basics will set you up for the rest of your life; golf is so much more fun when you're playing well.

BEFORE YOU START

It almost goes without saying that you cannot expect to hit a target if you point the gun in the wrong direction. Likewise, you cannot hit consistently good golf shots if your set-up is incorrect.

A SECURE POSTURE

Posture refers to the body angles you create at address (as you prepare to swing). Correct posture encourages a good shape to your swing. As you stand over the ball, you should feel ready to go, and poised to swing the club away from the ball. Good posture is a huge part of building a sound golf swing.

2 ◄ Bend forwards from the hips, allowing your hands and arms to hang down comfortably. Flex your knees and stick out your buttocks slightly. Keep your stance powerful, balanced, almost athletic.

1 ◄ Position your feet and stand upright, with a club resting by your side.

3 ◄ Now reach for the club (or have someone hand it to you), without altering any of the angles you have created, and just ground the club. It might feel a little strange at first, but you have now established the perfect posture for someone of your height and build.

CALM DOWN

Everyone gets nervous on the first tee — even professionals. Here are a few ways to help you keep calm. A good first tee shot is a real morale booster, so do all you can to get it right.

Go with a club you feel confident of hitting solidly and accurately. You do not have to reach for your driver, even if it is quite a lengthy hole. Use a lofted wood, or even a long iron, if that is what you feel comfortable with. Getting the ball in play – on the short grass – is your priority.

Once you are ready to tee off, make a conscious effort to grip lightly but securely. Your overriding thought then should be "rhythm". Think about rhythm and simply swinging smoothly to a balanced finish.

PERFECT PARALLEL ALIGNMENT

Parallel alignment is a key factor in good golf shots, and it works like this. Imagine a railway track running from your position to the target. The outer rail runs along the ball-to-target line, and this is where you should align your clubface. The inner rail runs along the line through your feet, and ends up just to the left of the target. If you line your feet and club along these imaginary tracks, you will be in perfect parallel alignment.

BALL POSITION

Parallel alignment is only part of the story. You must also have the ball positioned in the stance so that the club head collects it on the ideal path. The best ball position varies depending on which club you are hitting.

The relatively straight face of the driver means that you must sweep the ball away to achieve acceptable results. You therefore need the ball forward in your

CALM DOWN

▲ To calm down, first slow down. Take deep breaths, inhaling then exhaling slowly, prior to teeing up. Also try jiggling your hands a little, as if you were shaking water from them, to help ease the tension. These simple exercises will induce a feeling of calm.

stance – roughly opposite the inside of your left heel – so that the club reaches the bottom of its swing at impact.

Short irons are different. They call for a more descending angle of attack: the clubhead must be travelling downwards into impact to ensure that you achieve ideal ball-then-turf contact. With the short irons, therefore, the ball should be positioned back in your stance – about midway between your feet.

PERFECT PARALLEL ALIGNMENT

BALL POSITION

EQUIPMENT

Choosing the equipment for any sport should not be taken lightly. In golf, the implements you use can make a difference. Given the complexities of swinging a small clubhead around a metre, or several feet, at speeds of up to 190 kph (120 mph) with the intention of making contact with a little ball, make sure that your golf equipment is helping rather than hindering you.

CLUBS

Choosing a club from the array of designs on offer can be a bewildering experience, especially as each new development promises to transform your game. For the beginner, it can be a good idea to purchase second-hand — a well-cared-for set of good-quality used clubs is often a better buy than a new set of cheaper clubs. It is also worthwhile to take advice from a good coach or the club professional before making your choice. In the end, though, only you can decide what feels right for your shape, strength and style of play.

Low-numbered clubs send the ball farther, but do not lift it as much as high-numbered clubs. A high-numbered club also creates more backspin, which reduces roll on landing. Irons are numbered from 2 to 9. The 2-iron has its

▼ Putters come in a variety of shapes and sizes. Choosing a putter is often a matter of trial and error, experience and feel.

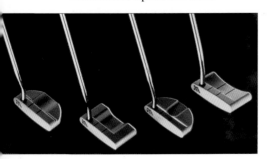

face angled at 18° from the vertical. This loft angle is increased by 4° for each higher numbered iron. The shaft also reduces in length as the club number increases, demanding a slightly higher swing plane. Woods are numbered from 1 to 5, with a 1-wood (or driver) usually having a loft from between 7° and 11°. An additional chipper will be invaluable for playing low-running balls.

▲ A standard club. You are allowed a maximum of 14 clubs in your bag, but beginners often make do with a 2-wood, a 3-, 5-, 7- and 9-iron, and a single wedge.

▲ Wood offers control and the ability to shape shots more readily, as well as a pleasing sound.

TRADITIONAL CLUBS

These clubs have most of the weight concentrated behind the middle of the clubface. This central area is known as the sweet spot, and a good, accurate strike here produces a penetrating, powerful flight. The disadvantage with these clubs is that a slight miss-hit gives a poor result.

PERIPHERAL-WEIGHTED CLUBS

Also known as cavity-backed or game-improvement club, these clubs have their weight distributed more evenly around the face, effectively increasing the size of the hitting area. If you hit a shot off the toe-end, for example, the result will not be too different to one struck from the middle. Hence, peripheral-weighted clubs are best for the beginner or inconsistent player — although they are valued by professionals too.

THE SHAFT

Shafts come in three flexes: soft, regular and stiff. As a rule, the better and stronger the player, the stiffer the shaft required. Shafts are usually made of steel or graphite. Steel is the preferred choice, but graphite offers significant benefits, at a price. Stronger but lighter than steel, graphite enables more mass to be concentrated in the clubhead where you need it most.

PUTTERS

Putting is open to greater personal interpretation than any other aspect of golf. Not surprisingly, therefore, the putter is available in a seemingly limitless variety of styles and designs. Most modern designs have the weight evenly distributed across the clubface, while many have a kink in the shaft just above the head to encourage your hands to lead the ball.

BALLS

Different types of ball are geared to players of different ability, although you should experiment with all types and choose the one that feels right for you.

THREE-PIECE BALLS

Professional players use a three-piece ball with a rubber centre, wound rubber interior and a separate outer cover. Some have a soft coating of rubber-like gum from the balata tree, which offers maximum spin rate and controllability at the expense of distance. These are chosen by skilled players concerned with feel, touch and control, but they are costly and easily damaged by a miss-hit. Other three-pieces come with a tougher synthetic (surlyn) cover, and give a reasonable level of controllability combined with resilience and distance. Most makes are also available in two levels of

▲ Before you buy a golf bag, fill it with clubs and test how it feels. Light-weight bags are perfect for summer, but many come without rain hoods, so carry a detachable one.

▼ Spiked soles are favoured for maximum stability in all weathers.

▼ Gloves can help you grip the club firmly. During wet weather, carry a few spares in a watertight plastic bag to keep your grip as dry as possible.

compression: 90 or 100. The 100 is slightly harder and is often used by stronger players.

TWO-PIECE BALLS

The two-piece ball has a solid rubber centre and a sturdy surlyn cover. Durable and tough, this ball drives the furthest, although at the expense of controllability. It is often used by beginners until they have developed their consistency and ball-control skills.

SHOES

You are likely to walk about 6.5 km (4 miles) per game, and climb up and down hills with a heavy bag, so comfortable, supportive, waterproof shoes are essential.

HAT

A peaked cap or visor keeps rain or sun off your face or spectacles.

UMBRELLA

A golfing umbrella should be large enough to cover your bag and yourself. Golfers often hang a towel from the spokes for drying hands or clubs.

THE PRE-SHOT ROUTINE

All good golfers have a consistent pre-shot routine: a series of moves that helps them assume the correct mental attitude, address position and good posture every time they stand to the ball before a shot.

THE ADDRESS POSITION

The address position is a rehearsal for the impact the clubhead is going to make with the ball. You cannot direct the golf ball in the correct direction if you are not positioned in readiness for the move. If you need convincing of the importance of the address position, study professionals in action and see how meticulous they are in this area. However accurate your stroke, it must be aimed in the right direction in order to find its mark.

A faultless set-up, or address position, is the first step to producing a good golf swing. Furthermore, the set-up is something over which even a beginner has total control. You will improve your chances of hitting the ball correctly by dedicating time and effort to positioning yourself advantageously.

DEVELOPING YOUR STYLE

When you have developed your own style, you will need to adjust your address position to take into account conditions of play, weather, course obstacles — and your own weaknesses and strengths. When you are in the first stages of learning, concentrate on developing a position that can be used under most circumstances, even by players with little experience. It is essential that you develop your own set-up routine, ideally based on the following principles.

1 ◀ Stand behind the ball and visualize the exact shot you want to hit. This helps you focus your mind on the task at hand while fixing the target line in your head.

2 ▶ Align the clubface square to the target line by identifying an intermediate target just in front of you, such as an old divot (dislodged turf) mark or a leaf. It is easier to aim the clubface at a close target than at an object some 200 metres or yards distant.

3 ▶ Secure your
hands comfort-
ably on the grip
and then build your
stance around the
clubface. Remember
that good posture
is paramount and
keep your knees
flexed while bending
forwards from the
hips. Try to get
everything square
to the bottom edge
of the clubhead –
in perfect parallel
alignment. Your
body alignment
determines the path
along which the
clubhead is swung
and is crucial to a
good shot.

4 ▶ Once you are
set, waggle the
clubhead back and
forth a couple of
times to ease the
tension in your
hands, arms and
shoulders. This
relaxation promotes
fluidity of move-
ment. Provided your
posture is also good,
you are now in great
shape to swing the
club correctly away
from the ball.

GRIP

The legendary golfer Ben Hogan summed it up when he said, "A player with a bad grip doesn't want a good swing." There are several ways of holding the club, and you should choose the one that feels most comfortable for you from the three leading recognised grip styles. This will largely depend on the size of your hands. The overlapping grip offers a high degree of control, if your hand span is large enough. The interlocking and baseball grips are strong alternatives for women players and juniors. Remember, without a good grip, your game has little hope of progressing.

PERFECT POSTURE: OVERLAPPING GRIP

In order for your hands to work in harmony during the swing, you need a good grip on the club. The overlapping grip, whereby the little finger of the right hand rests on top of the index finger of the left hand, is one of the most popular and effective grips in the game today, adopted by many of the world's best golfers. Your hands are your only contact with the club, so good contact is vital.

Align your head with your neck, looking towards the club

Hold your back in a straight line from neck to waist

Relax your arms and let them hang down comfortably

Bend your hips forward and stick out your rear end slightly

Hold your stomach firmly to support your back

Grip the club firmly with the bottom finger of your right hand overlapping with the top finger of your left hand

Bend your knees slightly

Position the club a comfortable distance from your feet in parallel alignment with the rest of your body

Position your feet hip-width apart and hold a firm, balanced stance

TECHNIQUE
OVERLAPPING GRIP

Today, the overlapping grip is by far the most popular method for holding the golf club. However, up to the turn of the century, it was almost unheard of.

THE "VARDON" GRIP

The overlapping grip is sometimes called the Vardon grip, in honour of the turn-of-the-century championship player Harry Vardon who did so much to spread its popularity. Vardon was by no means the first player to advocate this revolutionary new style – it was also used by his contemporaries and rivals, John H. Taylor and James Braid. Together with technical improvements such as a thinner grip on the shaft of the club and newer, faster golf balls, the overlapping grip changed the way the game was played. Its fast-increasing popularity led to a more modern, effective style of play, with a longer, more fluid golf swing and a greater degree of body movement than before. Without the freedom of movement that the new grip allowed, the golf swing that we take for granted today might never have developed.

THE GRIP OF CHAMPIONS

The overlapping grip is still the first choice of most professional players, who find that the contact between the hands means that they act in unison with each other. Club players too can benefit from the control and flexibility associated with this grip.

The following instructions show how to achieve the perfect grip. Left-handed players should reverse the instructions.

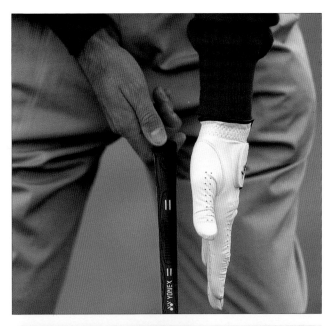

1 ◄ Support the top of the club with your right hand. Hang the left hand naturally down the side of the grip.

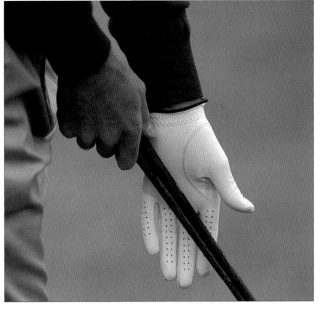

2 ◄ Bring your left hand forward from its natural hanging position and hold it against the grip in such a way that the shaft runs from the fleshy pad in your palm down diagonally through the middle joint of your index finger.

3 ◄ Now close the fingers of your left hand around the club.

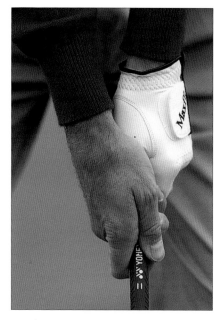

5 ◄ Bring your right hand forward and lay the club in the fingers of that hand. Try to imagine that your right palm coincides with the angle of the clubface; in other words, it is square to the target. Your right thumb and fore-finger should form a kind of trigger around the grip, almost to the extent that you can sup-port the weight of the club in your finger and thumb.

4 ◄ Your thumb should be flat on the grip, perhaps a little to the right of centre as you look down on it.

6 ◄ Bond the little finger of your right hand over the index finger of your left hand. Keeping the hands as close together as possible, as shown, allows optimum control over the swing.

TECHNIQUE
ALTERNATIVE GRIPS

The other two popular grips are the interlocking grip and the baseball grip. Golfers of all levels are traditionally lazy about their grip. Because it is not an exciting subject, the grip tends not to receive the attention that it warrants. Sadly, even many professional golfers who grip the club badly do so out of ignorance, but this could be corrected by just a few minutes' study.

THE INTERLOCKING GRIP

The interlocking grip is a slight variation on the overlapping grip. The right-hand little finger is entwined with the left-hand forefinger. Players with short fingers often favour this grip. Jack Nicklaus uses the interlocking grip to devastating effect. If it works for you, then do not hesitate to use it.

THE BASEBALL GRIP

Prior to this century, club shafts had very thick grips, so the baseball grip was the only possible – and recognized – method for holding the club. It remained the only recognized grip until the early years of the twentieth century, when the overlapping grip was first pioneered by ground-breaking players such as James Braid, Harry Vardon and John H. Taylor. The overlapping grip is now the dominant style. The baseball grip is by no means obsolete, however, and is particularly useful for younger players or those suffering from arthritis.

◀ INTERLOCKING GRIP
This grip tends to be favoured by golfers with relatively short fingers. The bottom finger of your right hand overlaps with the top finger of your left hand.

◀ BASEBALL GRIP
Sometimes called the two-handed grip, this grip is ideal for younger players or players who have arthritic problems. The two hands are positioned on top of each other.

POSSIBLE PITFALLS

◄ WEAK GRIP
Your grip is weak if your hands are turned too far round to the left. This will make it extremely difficult to return the clubface square to the ball at impact.

◄ STRONG GRIP
Your grip is strong if your hands are turned too far to the right. A slightly strong right-hand grip is acceptable, but from the front you should never be able to see more than three knuckles.

EXERCISE

HOW TO PERFECT YOUR GRIP

1 ◄ Your grip influences your impact position. Both hands should be in a neutral position. Here is a simple way to check that this is indeed the case. Stand in front of a mirror and slowly place each hand on the grip. First, the left hand. As you look at it, the "V" formed by the index finger and thumb should point up somewhere between your right eye and right shoulder.

2 ◄ Similarly with the right hand, the "V" should point to the same area between your right eye and right shoulder. If there is any deviation from this, your hands are in the wrong position.

SWING

American professional Tom Purtzer is credited by his fellow players as having the best swing in the world of golf. Before you can hope to achieve anything like such classic style, you need to study the basic components of the swing. A visit to any professional tournament provides ample evidence that there are many different ways to swing a golf club. But whatever technique they use, all good players have one thing in common: the consistent ability to deliver the clubhead correctly to the ball. If you can manage that, the aesthetics can take care of themselves.

PERFECT POSTURE: THE BACKSWING

In any shot, a good swing is half the battle. At the top of the backswing the shoulders should have turned 90 degrees and the hips 45 degrees, with the shaft of the club pointing on a line parallel to the target. In a powerful swing, the majority of bodyweight is supported over a flexed right knee, with the shaft of the club pointing on a line parallel to the target.

Swing club up over shoulder in one fluid movement

Keep the grip constant

Turn your head towards the ball

Turn the shoulders 90 degrees

Bring your left arm up and across the body

Turn the hips 45 degrees

Bend left knee slightly to keep your balance

Flex right knee and support your body weight over this knee

Position feet hip-width apart, with a firm stance

TECHNIQUE
THE BACKSWING

The swing is, to a large degree, a chain reaction. One good move generally leads to another. Make a mistake, though, and just as surely another mistake usually follows. That is why the first move away from the ball is so critical – it sets the pattern for your entire swing.

THE TAKEAWAY

The aim of the backswing is to position the clubface correctly. The takeaway is the beginning of the backswing. This must be a one-piece movement, with the left and right sides moving together. Throughout this part of the swing, your elbows should remain the same distance apart as they were at the address position, and you must keep the head of the club square with your shoulders. Ensure that your bodyweight is transferred smoothly on to the instep of your right foot. Keep the clubhead square to your shoulders during the swing, keep your left arm straight and avoid an early wrist cock when using long clubs. Remember to keep your head still, and your eyes on the ball.

CONTROL YOUR POWER

Most beginners make the mistake of aiming for maximum power, without learning how to control the direction of the ball. A truly great golfer knows that accuracy in a given shot is far more important than length. Practise your swinging movement in front of a mirror, paying attention to your club position and swing plane. Or get a friend to photograph you in action .

1 ◄ From a solid address position, your main thought should be to swing the club smoothly away from the ball, keeping your arms and body working in harmony.

2 ◄ This movement is referred to as the one-piece takeaway, and it is by far the most reliable method. The clubhead moves away low to the ground, gradually arcing inside the target line as the body rotates and the left arm extends away.

3 ◀ The wrists should hinge (or "set") in harmony with the swinging motion of the clubhead. Bear in mind that as the arms swing, so the body rotates. All components work together – your arms should never operate independently of the rest of your body.

POSSIBLE PITFALLS

1 ◀ There are two possible errors in club alignment that are sometimes introduced at the top of the swing. First, you can find yourself in a laid-off position, where the club points left of target.

4 ◀ As you reach the top of the backswing, your club should still be on line, parallel to the target.

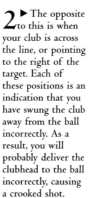
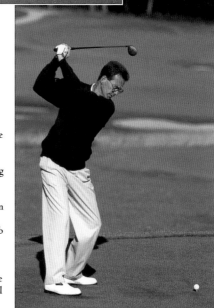

2 ▶ The opposite to this is when your club is across the line, or pointing to the right of the target. Each of these positions is an indication that you have swung the club away from the ball incorrectly. As a result, you will probably deliver the clubhead to the ball incorrectly, causing a crooked shot.

TECHNIQUE
THE DOWNSWING

The downswing is a reaction, not an action. Everything that happens depends upon what has gone before, which is why your grip, posture, alignment and backswing are so important. The downswing images shown here are positions within one continuous motion. You swing through these positions, not to them.

3 ◄ Now you are positioned to deliver the clubhead square to the back of the ball.

1 ◄ The transition period from the end of the backswing to the start of the downswing is critical. Try to feel that you start your downswing with a subtle move of your left knee towards the target, combined with a gradual weightshift on to your left foot. This is referred to as leg separation.

4 ◄ Through impact, your hands and arms freewheel up and around into the perfect follow-through position, which is the mark of a good player.

2 ◄ The move initiates an unwinding of your hips and torso, which automatically slots your hands and arms down into an ideal position to attack the ball from the inside.

5 ◄ By this stage, of course, it is far too late to influence the outcome of the shot. But it is a good idea to imagine yourself finishing in a balanced, poised position. It promotes an unhurried, controlled action and removes any tendency to swing too hard.

PERFECT POSTURE: THE DOWNSWING

The sequence of events, rather than the speed, is the secret to a great downswing.
If the weight moves towards the left side, the hips and upper body start to unwind,
which drops the hands, arms and club into the perfect downswing slot. Thus the
perfect transition from backswing to downswing is a chain reaction. Every link in
the chain that you perform correctly increases your chances of success at impact.

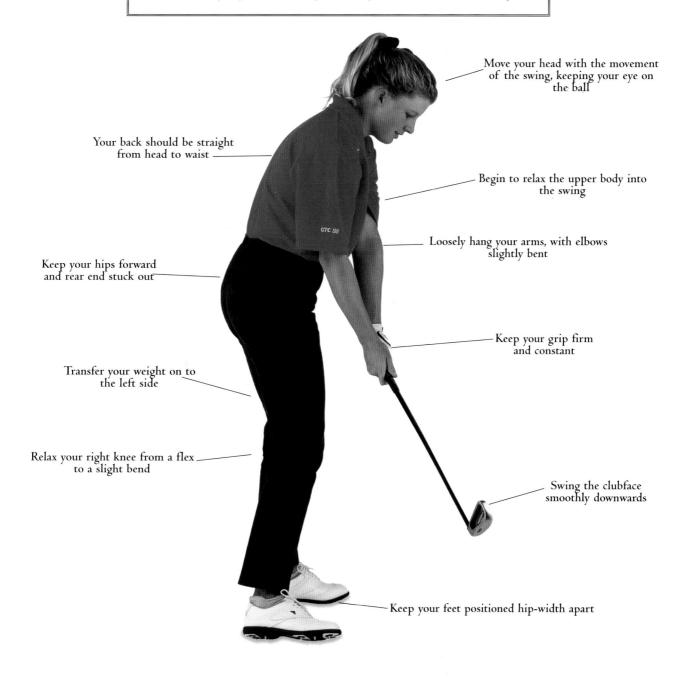

Move your head with the movement of the swing, keeping your eye on the ball

Your back should be straight from head to waist

Begin to relax the upper body into the swing

Loosely hang your arms, with elbows slightly bent

Keep your hips forward and rear end stuck out

Keep your grip firm and constant

Transfer your weight on to the left side

Relax your right knee from a flex to a slight bend

Swing the clubface smoothly downwards

Keep your feet positioned hip-width apart

POSSIBLE PITFALLS

WRONG LEG AND BODY ANGLES

INCORRECT FLEXION IN THE KNEES

1 ◄ Your legs are the foundation of your swing and, as in any structure, if the foundations are faulty, then the upper reaches tend to crumble. Learn to feel the correct amount of flex in your knees. Too much flex in the knees is rare, but it does happen.

INCORRECT BODY ANGLE

1 ◄ You must create the correct body angles at address before you can build a good swing. A good swing would be unlikely from this position.

2 ◄ Rigid, straight legs at address are a more familiar sight.

2 ◄ From this position it would be impossible to make a powerful turn away from the ball.

EXERCISE
TO CORRECT YOUR POSTURE

1 ◀ Address the ball normally, and then hold the shaft of a club along the length of your spine. Get used to the feeling of sticking your buttocks out slightly and matching the angle of your spine with the line of the shaft of the club.

2 ◀ Repeat this exercise as often as you like to familiarize yourself with the sensation that it brings. When you begin to feel more comfortable with the position, start to hit half-shots.

3 ▲ Once you have established a solid foundation, it will be easier to arrive in a good position at the top of the backswing and continue the good work from this position.

TECHNIQUE
CONTROLLING SWING PLANE AND TEMPO

How fast or slowly you swing the club is entirely an individual matter. The important point is that the rhythm remains constant from start to finish. Fast or slow is irrelevant – maintaining a consistent rhythm is all that matters. The ability to maintain a constant rhythm is the main factor separating tour professionals from handicap golfers. You need to find your own best pace at which to swing a club: a tempo that allows you to stay in control of your movements.

SHAPING YOUR SWING
The shape of your swing is determined by a combination of your height, build and the length of your arms. Provided you perfectly co-ordinate the turning motion of your upper body and the swinging motion of your arms, the swing plane will take care of itself.

The swing leads to the moment of impact. Impact is not something you swing to; it is something you swing through. Nonetheless, there are several highly effective ways of improving your impact position and thus the quality of your ball-striking. For a quick exercise, take two golf clubs of similar weight, such as a couple of mid-irons. Grip them in baseball fashion and assume a good golfing position. Swing the clubs simultaneously, back and forth, very slowly and very smoothly. In addition, the techniques and exercises on these pages will improve your movement.

1 ▲ The 9-iron has a much shorter shaft which obliges you to stand closer to the ball.

1 ▲ A long club, such as a driver, will require you to stand further away from the ball which will affect your swing plane.

2 ▲ From such a position as this, your swing will automatically become steeper and more upright.

2 ▲ This will cause you to have a fairly flat, shallow swing plane.

EXERCISE

GET YOUR SWING BACK ON TRACK

1 ◄ Address the ball as normal, only this time drag your left foot back so that your toe is level with your right heel. As you do this, it is important to try to keep your shoulder-line parallel to the target. Take a close look at your grip. Make sure you place your hands in a neutral position on the grip at address.

3 ◄ Instead of hitting the ball from way inside the line, which is what causes the hook, you'll start to train a more on-line downswing attack.

2 ◄ Your arm-swing is more in turn with your body rotation, which also results in a better position at the top of the backswing.

4 ◄ Having your left foot drawn back also forces you to clear your left side in the down-swing through impact – another factor which helps eliminate the damaging hook.

EXERCISE
ACHIEVING MAXIMUM DISTANCE

1 ◄ Hitting the ball long distances is a product of good technique – the reward for paying attention to the fundamentals of the swing. As the legendary teacher John Jacobs says, "Distance is achieved through clubhead speed correctly applied." One of the most common errors that cause loss of distance is chopping down on the ball much too steeply. This exercise can help you accentuate some of the key factors that cause the ball to fly further.

2 ▲ To prevent or cure this fault, practise hitting drives from an extra high tee-peg. Set up using your normal routine.

3◀ Make sure that you keep the clubhead hovering off the ground. If you were to chop down too steeply on a ball teed this high, you would miss it altogether.

5◀ Not only does this exercise help you to coil more effectively in the backswing, it also stops you from becoming too steep in the downswing and encourages you to sweep the ball away.

4◀ The extra height encourages you to sweep the clubhead away from the ball on a shallow arc, so that you make a more rounded, less up-and-down swing.

6◀ Practise this technique and you will strike the ball more solidly, which will have the desired result of making it travel further.

EXERCISE
ONE-ARMED SWING

1 ◄ Grip the hosel of any club with your right hand only. Here, a 7-iron is used.

3 ◄ Then really whip the club through the "hitting zone". Allow your body to respond to the motion of your arm and listen to the club as it whooshes through the air.

2 ◄ As you swing the grip-end back, make a good upper-body turn and feel your right arm fold as it should in the backswing.

4 ◄ This exercise enhances the feeling of straightening your right arm in the downswing – known as re-establishing the arc. It also encourages the correct release through impact, essential to good shot-making. As you become more familiar with this sensation, take the exercise a stage further and hit half-shots with your right hand only. Tee the ball up and remember to take hold towards the bottom of the grip, where your right hand usually rests.

EXERCISE

STRENGTHENING THE LEFT-ARM SWING

1 ◀ Take your 7-iron, but this time grip it with your left hand only, otherwise adopting a normal good golfing posture. Tuck your right hand in your pocket to keep it out of the way.

3 ◀ Feel the weight of the clubhead at the end of the shaft and accelerate smoothly through impact. If your grip is sound, the correct forearm rotation and wrist hinge will develop naturally in the swing.

2 ◀ Make a number of three-quarter swings, concentrating on maintaining a smooth, unhurried and even tempo.

4 ◀ The emphasis throughout this exercise is on "smoothly". If you try to hit these shots too hard you are likely to bring excessive body movement into the swing, and that defeats the object of the exercise. Worse, you might cause yourself an injury. So build up slowly, starting the exercise by hitting half-shots, if necessary. Alternatively, clip a tee-peg out of the ground until you feel the strength in your left arm is sufficient to begin hitting the ball.

PUTTING

There are a multitude of ways to putt, and no general consensus as to which is the right one. Ben Crenshaw, winner of the 1984 US Masters, is one of the greatest putters of all time. But even given the remarkable results that his stroke produces, describing only his method would tell an incomplete story. What we can do is offer you a variety of proven methods from which you can select the one that pops the ball into the hole most often. Devote time on the practice green to finding a technique that is right for you, and make it your own.

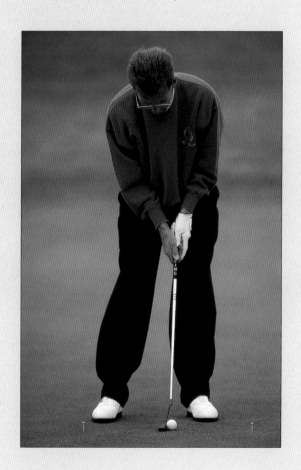

PERFECT POSTURE: PUTTING

In the perfect putting posture the hands and arms should hang naturally, free
from tension, to promote a free swing of the putter back and forth. The eyes
should be directly over the ball, offering the best possible view down the line
towards the hole. Putting is a shoulder and arms movement — there should be no
wrist action during the stroke.

Head bends forward to
keep the ball in view
with eyes directly over
the ball

Bend from your hips so that
you are leaning slightly over
the putter

Let your arms hang loosely in front
of your body, free from tension

Keep your wrists still, firmly
gripping the putter

Keep your keees
slightly bent

Don't move your feet — they
should be firmly planted on the
ground, hip-width apart

TECHNIQUE
BASIC PUTTING

Putting is open to great personal inter-pretation, but it pays to adhere to the fundamentals. If necessary, you can then adapt those basic principles to suit your own style.

PRACTICE MAKES PERFECT

Confidence in putting will come from good, sound technique and practice. Experiment with a variety of approaches until you find the one you are happiest with – when you are playing under pressure in competition, your labours will be rewarded.

It is always best to practise on a level part of the green: once you can make the ball race straight on short distances, then you will be able to cope with long putts and borrows in the green.

The most important part of any putt is the first 30 cm (12 in). If the putt starts correctly then there is a fairly good chance of success, but a putt that starts badly very rarely improves.

Having lined the ball with the centre of the clubface, practise making a smooth back and through swing striking the ball in the same spot – that is, the spot on the clubface that you lined up the ball with at the address.

Depending on the speed and the length of the green, the distance you have to swing the putter will vary. For putts of up to 15 cm (6 in) the putter head needs to go back in a straight line from the ball and hole. As the length of the putt increases, the length of the swing will also increase, and in so doing the putter will come back slightly on the inside.

1 ◀ If there is a classic putting stroke, this is probably it. Place the hands in a neutral position – the palms facing each other – in what is termed the reverse overlap grip. This encourages the hands to operate as a cohesive unit, rather than moving independently of each other.

2 ◀ Adopt a relaxed posture: a comfortable bend from the waist, with the hands and arms hanging down naturally and completely free from tension. Place the ball forward in your stance, roughly opposite the inside of the left heel. Stand with your eyes positioned over the ball, which allows you to swivel your head to look along the line of the putt.

3 ◀ The stroke itself is essentially a pendulum action, controlled predominantly by the shoulders, with the hands remaining fairly passive. Note the imaginary triangle formed by the arms and shoulders at address.

5 ◀ Concentrate on trying to swing the putter-head upwards into and through impact. Having the ball forward in your stance encourages that upward strike and promotes a good roll. A descending blow, on the other hand, tends to cause the ball to jump into the air.

4 ◀ Try to maintain that triangular relationship throughout the stroke, from backswing to final follow-through.

6 ◀ Hold your follow-through position and do not look up too soon. Keep your eyes on the ground until the ball is well on its way. Hopefully, you will be greeted with the sight of the ball dropping gently into the hole.

POSSIBLE PITFALL

THE ANTI-YIP STROKE: DROPPING THE LEFT HAND

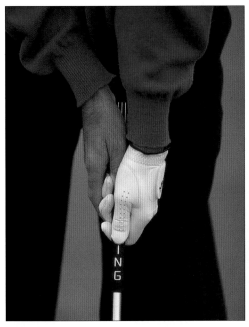

1 ▲ In putting, allowing the left wrist to break down through impact is referred to as "the yips". This causes the putter-face to behave erratically. A basic anti-yip technique is to grip the club with your left hand below the right. This locks the left wrist into position against the shaft of the putter and prevents any unwanted wrist action in the stroke.

2 ▶ This grip also has the added advantage of lowering the left shoulder, bringing it more into line with the right.

3 ◄ In other respects, the stroke closely resembles the more orthodox action described in Basic Putting.

5 ▲ Note again how the left wrist remains firm through the ball – there is no breakdown whatsoever in this area.

4 ◄ The shoulders control the motion – simply rock them back and forth to regulate the necessary force in the stroke.

POSSIBLE PITFALL

LOOKING UP TOO SOON

1 ◀ Set up a medium-range putt and address the ball. Now close your eyes. One of the biggest causes of missed putts is looking up too soon. If you move your head too soon, your whole upper body moves with it, which effectively drags the putter-face left of target.

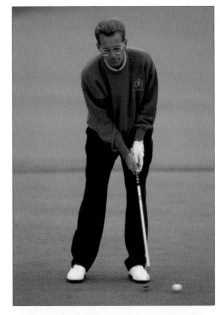

3 ◀ This prevents you from becoming too preoccupied with hitting at the ball and, more importantly, helps you to concentrate on making a smooth stroke.

2 ◀ Keeping your eyes closed, stroke the ball towards the hole.

4 ◀ Again smoothness is important. Your stroke should not be a jab at the ball. The perfect stroke is one that takes the putter back low and slow, smoothly accelerating through impact. The ball merely gets in the way. Looking up too soon is usually a result of anxiety. Practise not looking up until you hear the ball dropping into the hole. Your stroke is guaranteed to stay on line for longer – and to drop in the hole a lot more often than before.

POSSIBLE PITFALL
DECELERATION THROUGH IMPACT

▶ A smooth continuous action is essential, but the pressure of trying to get the ball into that tiny hole can cause you to tense up or rush your shot. However short the putt, or however fast the green, you must accelerate the putter-head into the back of the ball to hole out on a consistent basis. Always ensure that your through swing is exactly the same length as your backswing. Then concentrate on smoothly accelerating the putter through the ball.

The length of your backswing is crucial to striking good putts. The most destructive error of all is taking the club back. You then tend to decelerate the downswing and jab the ball with no follow-through. The ball is unlikely to approach the hole, let alone drop into it.

1 ▲ Try this practice exercise. Place two tee-pegs in the ground the same distance either side of your ball. The longer the putt, the longer the clearance you need between the ball and the tee-pegs.

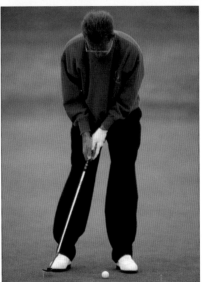

2 ▲ Hit some putts and use the tee-pegs to regulate the length of your stroke.

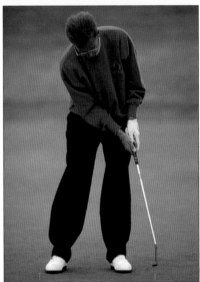

3 ▲ Concentrate on smoothly accelerating the putter-head through impact, whilst making sure that your backswing is exactly the same length as your follow-through.

TECHNIQUE
THE "LANGER" GRIP: KEEPING THE WRIST LOCKED

Bernhard Langer has made this method his own, and it is the culmination of years of frustration trying to overcome the yips. The method is best suited to short-range putting and is less effective from long distances.

1 ◄ Assume a comfortable stance and place the putter-head behind the ball, aiming the clubface using your right hand only.

2 ▲ Reach down with your left hand, gripping the club in a fairly orthodox manner and clasp the fingers of your right hand around your left forearm, as if you were taking your own pulse. This effectively takes the right hand out of the stroke.

3 ◄ Again, the ideal ball position is opposite the inside of your left heel. Make sure that your grip pressure is light. Any tension applied here will prevent a smooth, repeating stroke.

4◄ Now simply concentrate on rocking your shoulders back and through. This should provide all the force in the stroke.

6◄ The putter should move back and through in a straight line, staying square throughout with no interference from your hands.

5◄ The hands remain fairly passive and there is no wrist action whatsoever.

TECHNIQUE
USING THE LONG PUTTER

This specially modified long putter aroused much controversy when Sam Torrance first used it in the late 1980s. Although it looks a little strange, there are benefits to this style, which hinges on the principle of recreating a perfect pendulum motion with the putter.

1 ▼ Grip the club in your left hand at the top of the putter. Place against your chin or chest, depending on the length of the shaft.

2 ◄ Now you simply need to grip the club lightly in your right hand, in a similar way to a pencil, and rock the putter-head smoothly back and forth.

3 ◄ The beauty of this method is that you let the weight and momentum of the putter do all the work for you. And the fact that the right hand guides the stroke means that there is no chance of your hands working independently of one another.

4 ◄ The method improved Sam Torrance's consistency – and you never know, it could work for you.

EXERCISE
DEVELOP A SQUARE PUTTING STROKE

1 ◄ While on longer putts the putter-head naturally travels back inside the line, it's not the case from short range. Ideally, the putter-head should travel square-to-square – use straight back and straight through, with the putter-face staying square to the target-line throughout. This exercise is designed to channel a square-to-square putting stroke. Identify a straight putt and place two blocks of wood on the ground in such a way that they form a channel towards the hole. Place a ball between the two blocks and line up the putter-face squarely to the hole. There should be roughly a 1.5 cm (½ in) gap either side of the toe and heel of the putter.

3 ◄ Provided you align the putter-face correctly, you cannot miss. You need not use blocks of wood, of course. The shafts of two golf clubs or a pair of flag sticks are equally effective. Spend a couple of hours a week working on this exercise, and you will be amazed at the improvement to your holing out.

2 ◄ Now hit putts, making sure that neither the toe nor heel of the putter touches the blocks of wood – just swing it straight back and straight through.

EXERCISE

DEVELOP A FOOL-PROOF PUTTING STROKE

1 ◄ Repetition is the key to this exercise. Its purpose is to make you familiar with holing out from short range so that it becomes as routine as you can possibly make it. Obviously there is more pressure on the course, but this exercise helps prepare you for those stresses. Set out as many balls as you like in the form of a cross, starting 30 cm (12 in) from the hole and working out to a distance of no more than 1.5 m (5 ft). Now set yourself the target of holing each ball in succession, either by working away from the hole along one line at a time or by holing the four nearest balls, followed by the four second-nearest and so on. Whichever method you choose, keep to a consistent pattern.

2 ► If you miss one, whatever stage of the exercise you have reached, you must start all over again. Be strict with yourself. This exercise loses its purpose if you do not punish your misses. When you approach the end of the exercise without having missed a putt, you will begin to know what pressure is like. And the more you learn to cope with that feeling, the fewer putts you will miss in a competitive round. Practise your putting with the same type of ball as you would use on the course. Becoming accustomed to the feel of a particular ball is crucial in learning to judge the distance of your putts consistently.

EXERCISE

PUTTING WITH A SAND-WEDGE

1 ◄ A different but effective way to improve your putting is to practise with a sand-wedge. Hold the wedge slightly high, with the clubhead hovering level with the ball's equator.

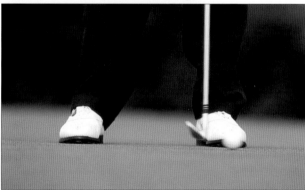

2 ◄ Concentrate on striking the ball on the up. The key is to strike the ball right on its equator to promote a smooth roll.

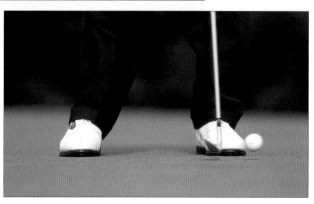

3 ◄ If the ball jumps at impact, you have made a bad stroke. As your confidence grows, revert to making the same stroke using your putter.

CHIPPING

At club level much emphasis is placed on the importance of building a sound golf swing, but this worthwhile goal is often sought at the expense of the short game. This is certainly not the case at the highest level. A player such as Colin Montgomerie will probably devote as much time to working on the short game as he will to the full swing. He knows that the sheer variety of situations that can occur in a tournament can test his chipping skills to the extreme. For players of all levels, close to the green is an area where imagination and versatility are both essential qualities.

One sentence captures the essence of good address position for chipping: "place the ball back and the hands and weight forward". This encourages the necessary crisp strike that is so much a part of a tidy short game. Once you have achieved the correct posture and made yourself familiar with the techniques, then, through practice you can develop your feel for those invaluable shots around the green.

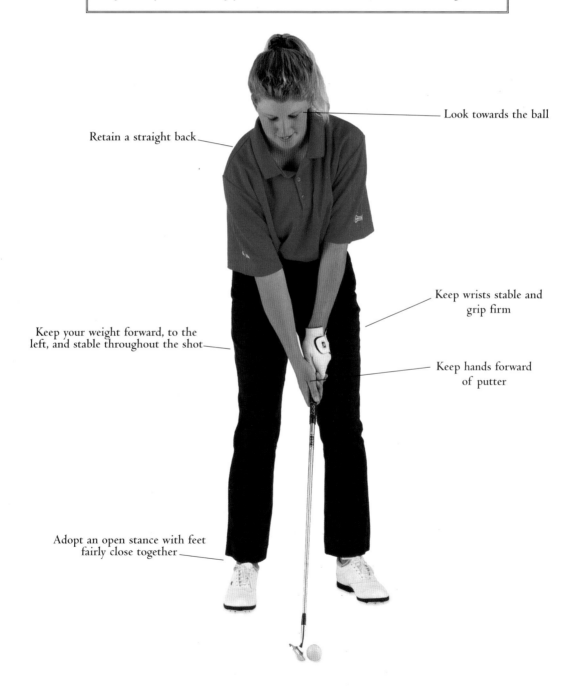

Look towards the ball

Retain a straight back

Keep wrists stable and grip firm

Keep your weight forward, to the left, and stable throughout the shot

Keep hands forward of putter

Adopt an open stance with feet fairly close together

TECHNIQUE

THE BASIC CHIP

Successful chipping calls for a solid technique as well as a keen awareness of the feel factor: the ability to judge flight, bounce and roll.

DISTANCE

The chip can be played from various distances on the putting surface, when you need a low running ball rather than a high ball. You can use your putter for this shot but often the fairway or the approach to the green is too wet, or not smooth enough to roll the ball over. The ideal club is a 4-iron, but as the shot is played with the ball quite close to your feet and the 4-iron shaft is quite long, it might get caught in your clothing. To avoid this, use a 6- or a 7-iron.

THE PERFECT CHIP

The chip is a low running shot, so you need to take loft off the clubface. At the address, set your hands slightly ahead of the ball, to deloft the ball. The clubface is now hooded. On the takeaway, there is no wrist break, the clubhead is still hooded, the body stays steady and the clubhead close to the ground. Master the basic chip first. You will then discover that the same technique can be applied to a number of different clubs, creating a whole repertoire of shots for various situations. With chipping, particularly over sand, the natural tendency is often to become so concerned with height that you scoop at the ball in an attempt to help it into the air. But remember the old golfing adage: "You've got to hit down to create height."

1 ◀ As with every golf shot, your address position is a vital factor. Adopt an open stance with your feet fairly close together and your weight favouring the left side. A useful guideline is, "ball back, hands forwards and weight forward".

2 ◀ Keeping your weight exactly where it is, make a compact backswing.

3◄ Wrist break is minimal: just a slight hinging, or setting, of the wrists as you complete the backswing. This effectively keeps the hands in charge, in an ideal position to lead the clubhead down into the ball.

4◄ At impact, you should feel that the ball is compressed between the clubface and turf. It is this sensation of squeezing the ball forward towards the target that helps produce the necessary backspin. With a lofted club you can expect a good deal of check-spin to retard the ball on the second or third bounce.

5◄ Remember that your hands should stay ahead of the clubhead even through impact. This technique is very versatile and can be used to good effect with your 7-iron, 9-iron and sand-wedge. Through the combination of experience and practice, you will soon learn which clubs perform best in certain situations.

TECHNIQUE

THE HIGH-FLOATING LOB

This is a shot that you should only ever play if you have no option — the classic example being when there is a bunker between your ball and the flag. When there is plenty of green, use one of the other safer shots that are better suited to the task. Although tricky, the high-floating lob is a shot that just might be a game winner.

2▲ Take your sand-wedge and align the clubface a little to the right of the target. This is termed an open club. Position the ball forward in your stance, roughly opposite the left heel.

3◀ Now for the swing itself. Keep your arm-swing in tune with your body rotation away from the ball, allowing your wrists to hinge gradually all the way through the backswing. This sets you on a fractionally steeper plane than normal. You may only have a short distance to cover, but you must still make a relatively long swing, both back and through the ball.

1▲ The high-floater is virtually the same as playing from a green-side bunker. First, you need to align your feet, hips and shoulders a little to the left of the target. This is known as an open stance.

4 ◄ On the way down, maintain the same smoothly accelerating action and almost slide the clubhead through the grass under the ball.

6 ◄ The combination of an open clubface and an out-to-in swing path produces a shot that flies straight at the target. Played correctly, the ball will pop high into the air and land softly – perfect when you have very little green to work with.

5 ◄ Do not allow any wrist action to creep in; as you rotate your body out of the way through impact, keep your left wrist firm and your right hand under the shaft to ensure that the clubface does not close.

TECHNIQUE

THE PUTT-CHIP

This is a useful variation on the standard chip shot: part-chip and part-putt. It is much simpler than it sounds; it is most useful when you have a relatively short distance — say, under 20 metres or yards — but the ground between your ball and the green is a little bumpy.

3 ◄ Make a fairly brisk action and clip the ball away.

1 ◄ Take a fairly lofted club, such as an 8- or 9-iron, and set up to the ball as if you were preparing to hit a long putt. Place your weight over on the left side and position the ball opposite your left heel. Remember to adopt your normal putting grip. This helps deaden the impact and enables you to control the length of the shot more accurately.

4 ◄ The ball is lobbed gently forwards. It is fairly low and with plenty of run.

2 ◄ Now simply go ahead and focus on executing an extension of your normal putting stroke.

5 ◄ It will race towards the hole, just like a long putt.

TECHNIQUE
THE CHIP FROM HARD GROUND

The bare lie on hard ground is perhaps the most feared shot, because it gives you so little margin for error and calls for precise technique.

THE RIGHT TOOLS

Your sand-wedge is totally unsuited to playing off a bare lie. The wide flange on the sole of the club raises the leading edge off the ground just a fraction, which is perfect for sand shots; from a bare lie, though, it tends to cause you to clip the top of the ball. So always use a club that has a sharper leading edge, such as a 9-iron. The leading edge sits tighter to the ground and enables you to execute the shot more precisely. Playing off a bare lie demands that you accentuate all the maxims and techniques that relate to the normal chip.

1▲ On a bare lie, the phrase "ball back, hands forward and weight forward" is even more critical. You need to exaggerate each of these three factors by another 20 per cent, so that the ball is well back in your stance and your hands and weight favour the left side even more than normal.

3▲ Once again, the single crucial aspect of the shot is to keep your hands ahead of the clubhead into, and through, impact.

▲ A 9-iron is the best club for the chip from hard ground. It will allow you to shape and direct your shot better than a sand-wedge.

2▲ Make a compact backswing with a hint of wrist-break, and smoothly accelerate the clubhead into the bottom of the ball.

4▲ If you can always achieve those impact factors, bare lies should hold few fears for you.

EXERCISE
DEVELOPING YOUR FEEL FACTOR

1 ◄ This exercise recreates an "on-course" situation. You only get one chance at each shot during a round of golf, so it is useful to put yourself under similar pressure when you practise. Select one spot on the practice ground and drop a dozen or so balls down beside you. For each shot, really focus on your intended landing area, almost to the exclusion of all else. That is your intermediate target. Then go ahead and play the shot. Chip each ball to a different target every time, all within a range of 20 to 50 metres or yards. The important point is only to make one attempt at each shot.

2 ► If you do not have a practice green, use head covers as targets. The purpose of the exercise is to grow accustomed to visualizing each shot before you play it. Select a landing area and predict the amount of run on the ball required, then match the club to fit your assessment. Experiment with any club between your 7-iron and sand-wedge.

POSSIBLE PITFALLS

1 ◄ The ball is positioned too far forward in the stance. The hands are behind the ball, too, which is bound to cause further problems. This awkward address position is bound to make matters worse.

2 ◄ Impact becomes a scooping action with the clubhead travelling upwards into the middle of the ball, sending it scuttling along the ground. The effort to create height produces the exact outcome it sought to avoid – a bunker shot before the next putt!

EXERCISE

AVOIDING SCOOPING THE BALL

1 ◄ Always trust the loft on the clubface to do the job it was designed to do. Set up the shot with the ball in the centre of your stance and your hands comfortably ahead of that point. As a quick check, your left arm and the shaft of the club should form an approximately straight line down to the ball.

2 ◄ Once you have established that relationship at address, you must maintain it throughout the swing. The hands lead the clubhead into the ball to encourage a crisp, downward strike. This utilizes the effective loft on the clubface and ensures that you create height on the shot. Soon you will find that those embarrassing fluffed chips are a thing of the past.

PITCHING

Pitch shots are the in-between shots: longer than a chip, but shorter than a full swing. For this reason, they are often played badly. Rather than attacking the pin as they should, many golfers miss the green altogether. José Maria Olazabal is highly effective from inside 100 metres (100 yards), not merely hitting greens but aiming to hole every shot. As Gary Player once observed, 70 per cent of all shots in a round of golf are played within 70 metres (70 yards) of the green: all the more reason to develop a reliable technique in this crucial area of the golf course.

Look towards the ball

Maintain square shoulders

**Bend your body at the
hips and stick out your
rear end**

Relax arms and let them hang
down naturally

**Bend your knees slightly
as in the classic address
position**

**Stand with a slightly open stance
and keep balanced throughout
the shot**

TECHNIQUE
THE BASIC PITCH SHOT

This is the shot you would use at distances from 70 to 100 metres/yards. Having established the correct address position, you are now ready to make a good swing. It can help to imagine a three-quarter swing, back and through, and to keep that image in mind while you play the shot.

The pitch is used when you need the ball to fly high in the air over a hazard, such as a bunker or a bank. A lofted club – the sand- or pitching-wedge – is used to give the ball lift. Your choice of club will depend on the lie of the ball and the distance to the target. The pitching wedge is the more versatile of these two clubs because the sand-wedge must only be used in a bunker or on a soft, grassy lie.

BALL-TURF CONTACT

Striking with the pitching or sand-wedge is known as ball-turf contact. This is achieved with the correct movements of the lower body weight, and the arms and club on the downswing and through impact. It is important that you do not let the club overtake your arms as you hit the ball. You must never try to lift the ball off the ground up into the air; use the loft on the clubface instead.

As in the chip, the feel of the shot is of enormous importance. The pitch is what is called a "pressure" shot because it is a chance for you to improve your score. The likelihood of an error is small – if you fail to send the ball high it may also end up in a bunker.

1 ◄ Use your arms and shoulders to swing the club away from the ball in conjunction with the turning motion of your upper body.

2 ◄ Everything moves away together. Sometimes referred to as "staying connected in the backswing", this is a far more reliable method than if your hands and arms worked independently from the rest of your body.

3 ◄ Your body rotation should control the length of your backswing, and you need to keep your arms working in harmony to maintain that relationship.

5 ◄ Accelerate the clubhead down into and through impact, with the emphasis on the body, not the hands.

4 ◄ Similarly, in the downswing you should consciously make the arms and body control the swing together. Your hands need to stay fairly passive.

6 ◄ Practise this technique with a number of clubs – for example, your 9-iron, pitching-wedge and sand-wedge. This will enable you to use exactly the same swing without any conscious manipulation, while varying the distance you can hit the ball.

TECHNIQUE
PITCHING FROM DEEP ROUGH

This is a situation that all golfers face a little more often than they would wish – your ball is buried in the rough. Certainly, some strokes are impossible out of the rough, but there is no reason why you cannot set yourself up for a holeable putt. The most important point is to create a steeper angle of attack in order to make the best possible contact with the ball.

◀ Hover the club-head off the ground just a fraction. This will help you hit the ball as cleanly as possible at impact.

I ◀ The key to pitching from a deep rough is to position the ball further back in your stance. That way, the clubhead naturally achieves impact before it reaches the bottom of its swing arc, thus minimizing the amount of grass trapped between the club-face and the ball.

2◄ Once you have pre-set this steep angle of attack, take a slightly shorter club than you would use from the same distance on the fairway and slide or "choke" your hands down on the grip.

3◄ Now make a compact, three-quarter backswing.

4◄ You need to make sure that you punch the club-head down into the back of the ball.

5◄ Do not expect to generate backspin out of the rough – it is just not possible – so allow for more run on the ball than you would with a shot from the fairway.

TECHNIQUE
THE WIND CHEATER

If either your swing or your strategy is vulnerable, wind has a nasty habit of exposing those weaknesses. Most golfers try to hit the ball harder, but this creates excessive spin and lift on the ball, which is further exaggerated by the wind. When the wind is blowing hard, the key to keeping your scores low is to keep the ball low.

Controlling the Distance
The main difficulty that most people have with pitching shots is judging and controlling the distance they shoot. A common fault is when players make the same length of backswing for all pitch shots and attempt to regulate distance by varying the amount of force they exert in the downswing. This is an extremely haphazard way of controlling distance and tends to produce inconsistent shots. What you must appreciate is that the length of your backswing should directly relate to the distance the ball flies.

The Right Tools
First establish whether you are dealing with a one-club, two-club or three-club wind. Select your club accordingly and choke down 2 to 5 cm (1 to 2 in) on the grip. Judging the strength of the wind, and the effect it has on your ball, is a lesson you can only learn through experience. If you are not certain, do not worry – it will come in time.

1 ◄ Place the ball centrally in your stance with your hands ahead of the clubhead, perfect for punching the ball out on a low trajectory. Shift your weight slightly over to the left side – a ratio of 60 to 40 is ideal. Remember, your feet should be aligned to the left of the target.

2 ◄ Make a compact, three-quarter backswing with a little less hinging of the wrists than you would normally apply.

3 ◄ Keep your swing nicely rounded, again with your arms and body working in unison. Do not transfer your weight as much as you would for a full shot. Keep it centred over the ball.

5 ◄ Note how the follow-through is the same length as the backswing: a very constructive image to have in mind. And remember, "in the breeze, swing with ease". The harder you hit the ball, the more backspin you generate and the higher the ball climbs.

4 ◄ Now, from a three-quarter position, make sure your hands lead the clubhead down towards the ball. Rotate your upper body and try to keep the clubhead travelling low to the ground through impact and around into a balanced finish.

EXERCISES
CONTROLLING DISTANCE

1 ◄ This exercise gives you a feeling of how the length of swing relates to the distance you actually hit the ball. You can apply it to a variety of clubs – for example, to give you two different length pitch shots with your 9-iron. The best way to visualize this is to imagine that there are four "gears" to your swing. First gear is the short chip shot.

3 ◄ Third gear is the pitching gear for longer shots. Remember that the length of your backswing should directly relate to the distance the ball flies.

2 ◄ Second gear is the gear you use for pitching short shots.

4 ◄ In fourth gear you let fly with full swing.

1◄ Hit ten half-shots with your wedge – in second gear.

3◄ Now hit ten three-quarter shots – third gear. Again note the average "air time" for each one.

2◄ Make sure the follow-through is as long as the backswing. Take note of the average distance your shots travel.

4◄ Practise this exercise as often as you can until your second and third gears achieve a reasonable level of consistency. The next time you are on the course and you have, for instance, 75 metres (75 yards) to the flag, you can say to yourself, "OK, this is third gear with my sand-wedge". This exercise will remove the guess-work from your game, replacing it with more construc-tive thoughts.

BUNKER PLAY

Most club golfers see bunker play as an unknown quantity, and for some, the sand is a trap with no means of escape. It is important to work on this area of your golf, because bad bunker play can breed negative thinking throughout your game. As top-class golfers like Ernie Els know, it is possible to recover your position from the sand and turn it to your advantage. Always rake the bunker after you have made your escape, to ensure that the surface is smooth for the next poor unfortunate player who follows you there.

PERFECT POSTURE: BUNKER PLAY

The key word in sand is "open". That means an open clubface, therefore pointing right of the flag, and an open stance, which means the feet, hips and shoulders are aligned left of the flag. This promotes an out-to-in swing path, an essential require-ment for good bunker play. Keep a firm hold on the club, look at the top of the ball and make a smooth, balanced swing.

Shoulders are aligned left of the target

Keep your eyes looking at the top of the ball

Hips are aligned to the left of the target

Secure your footing in the sand

Keep your stance open and slightly wider than usual

The clubface remains open

TECHNIQUE
REGULAR SPLASH SHOT

One of the keys to becoming a better bunker player is understanding that the bounce effect created by the specially designed sole on the sand-wedge is best utilized when the clubface is open – i.e. aligned to the right of your target. So your set-up is crucial.

THE PERFECT SET-UP
You need to open your stance by aligning your body, especially your hips, shoulders and feet, to the left of the target. Shuffle your feet down into the sand firmly to provide a secure footing and adopt a slightly wider stance than normal – try to feel settled over the ball. Take your grip, but make sure that the clubface is open in relation to your stance and is pointing a little to the right of the target.

1 ◄ Set up as described opposite, paying particular attention to your open stance.

2 ◄ Take the club back initially along the line of your feet, keeping the open alignment of the clubface.

3 ◀ Now for the swing itself. Keep your arm-swing in tune with your body rotation away from the ball, allowing your wrists to hinge gradually all the way through the backswing. This sets you on a fractionally steeper plane than normal. You may only have a short distance to cover, but you must still make a relatively long swing, both back and through the ball.

5 ◀ The open clubface combined with an out-to-in swing path sends the ball floating straight towards the flag. That is the mark of good bunker play: having the confidence to splash the clubhead into the sand at the correct angle of descent, trusting the design of the club to do the rest for you.

4 ◀ In the down-swing, you must smoothly accelerate the clubhead through the sand under the ball. This creates a splash effect, although you do not need to remove great quantities of sand.

6 ◀ As a useful guide to the length and force of the swing required, imagine you are playing a shot from the fairway twice as long as the one facing you in the sand. So for a 9 m (30 ft) bunker shot, you need the force of an 18 m (60 ft) pitch. This will compensate for the cushioning effect of the sand at impact.

TECHNIQUE
EXPLODING FROM THE BURIED LIE

This is the one situation where you can disregard the normal bunker shot rules. Playing from a plugged, or buried, lie calls for changes to your club, your address position and your swing. With lots of application, and a little bit of luck, you'll hit your fair share of these shots pretty close to the hole.

When the ball is buried, you need to use your pitching-wedge, not your sand-wedge. Here you want the clubhead to dig into the sand underneath the ball, and the relatively sharp leading edge of your pitching-wedge is better suited to that task.

1 ◄ Choose a sand-wedge for this shot. The design of the sand-wedge encourages the clubhead to slide through sand.

2 ◄ Do not open the clubface at address, and do not open your stance. Instead, stand square to the target, with the clubface square and with the ball back in your stance, towards the right foot.

3 ◄ With all the elements of a good set-up in place, you need to commit yourself to being fairly aggressive with this shot. On the backswing, pick the clubhead up a little more steeply than you would for a normal bunker shot.

4 ◄ Concentrate on striking down into the sand behind the ball. Ensure that your left wrist stays rock solid through impact, and do not hesitate to hit down hard.

5 ◄ A lot of sand will be lifted, so you must generate a great deal of for-ward momentum to enable the ball to clear the front lip of the bunker.

6 ▲ The ball is bound to come out low and it is impossible to generate backspin, so allow for plenty of run from a buried lie.

TECHNIQUE

THE FAIRWAY BUNKER: MAXIMIZING THE DISTANCE

The fairway bunker shot, where you have to cover a long distance, is unlike any other shot from sand. In many ways it is just like playing a shot from the fairway, except that there is a greater emphasis on the necessity to strike the ball cleanly. You cannot afford to let sand come between the clubface and the ball. Your priority is to clear the front lip of the bunker. Once you have chosen the correct club to do this, you can assess whether or not you can reach the target. If you cannot, do not be tempted to try a longer club – just settle for progressing the ball well down the fairway.

1 ◀ Take your chosen club choke down 2 to 5 cm (1 to 2 in) on the grip. This increases the likelihood of perfect contact, while adding the benefit of shortening your swing and enhancing your control of the ball.

▼ Your feet should be firmly bedded into the sand for a secure stance.

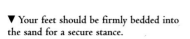

2 ◀ With the ball positioned in the centre of your stance, commit yourself to making a controlled, three-quarter swing from a solid stance.

3 ◄ If your feet are settled securely down into the sand, this will naturally steady your leg action and help make your swing tidy and compact.

5 ◄ You will then be back on the move again, having negotiated a hazardous bunker without falling behind in your score.

4 ◄ If you have chosen your club wisely, and executed the shot in a controlled fashion, you will clip the ball cleanly, with the merest puff of sand through impact.

POSSIBLE PITFALL

DIGGING TOO DEEP

1 ◀ Brute force will not dislodge a ball from the sand. If you try to blast the ball out in a great spray of sand, the results will be disastrous. Providing the lie is good, there is no need to employ muscle tactics to escape from a bunker. Without a solid grasp of the correct technique, you try to hit the ball too hard, which causes you to fall back on to your right foot. From here you either "thin" the ball or punch into the sand and catch it heavy.

2 ▶ The end result is usually the same, however you make contact. The ball remains in the sand, causing you to drop a shot and creating feelings of anger and frustration. A vicious circle often develops, with your trying to hit the ball even harder at the next attempt.

EXERCISE

THINK OF A "U" SHAPE

1 ◀ Try to visualize the clubhead travelling on a U-shaped path into and through impact. Take the club back, as in the classic bunker swing, hinging your wrists to set the club on a slightly steeper backswing plane.

3 ◀ You can now swing the clubhead down and through the sand on a much shallower angle of attack, thus achieving more consistent contact.

4 ▼ Instead of digging deep into the bunker, the clubhead splashes in and out of the sand, which has a kind of cushioning effect, throwing the ball out on a high-flying, soft-landing trajectory.

2 ◀ From here, start the downswing by shallowing the angle of the shaft, which causes the club to move into a slightly more horizontal position.

EXERCISE

PRACTISE IN THE SAND

1 ◄ Like all aspects of golf, good bunker play comes through a knowledge of the correct techniques and a commitment to practise what you learn. This exercise will help you visualize the correct contact you need to make in the sand. Line up four or five balls in a row and draw two lines on either side – one about 5 cm (2 in) in front of the balls and another the same distance behind them.

2 ◄ Now play each shot. Splash the clubhead down into the sand on the first line and imagine the clubhead coming out of the sand on the exact spot where you drew the second line. This helps remove the tendency to dig too deep and also encourages you to swing through the sand under the ball.

3 ◄ You can even try this action without the ball, just to get used to the feeling of splashing the clubhead through the sand. Once you are familiar with that sensation, play real shots and simply let the ball get in the way of your swing.

EXERCISE

THE UPHILL EXPLOSION SHOT

1 ◄ The key factor when playing from any kind of slope is to compose your set-up in such a way that you can make as normal a swing as possible. In sand, the same principle applies. Lodge your feet into the sand as high up the slope as you can comfortably manage, with your weight settled back over your right knee. Ideally, your shoulders should now be at the same angle as the slope, and the ball opposite the inside of your left heel.

3 ◄ Do not lean into the slope – you will only bury the clubhead so deep into the sand that the ball travels no distance at all. The combination of the upslope, your altered set-up and the shape of your swing ensures that the ball pops up high into the air and stops on landing almost at once. Don't worry too much about over-shooting the target. Try to land the ball on top of the flag-stick, which will help prevent you from leaving the ball well short.

2 ◄ Now focus on a spot roughly 5 cm (2 in) behind the ball and commit yourself to splashing the clubhead down into the sand on that exact spot.

Keep your weight back on your right side and make sure that the clubhead swings up the slope, through the sand and out.

SHAPING YOUR SHOTS

Manoeuvring the ball through the air is an advanced technique. Seve Ballesteros is the master — but all good players shape their shots. Two main factors dictate the flight of the ball: the alignment of the clubface at impact, and the path of the swing into and through impact. This section will help you understand and use these factors, to escape from trouble and improve your strategy. Not only will you be able to manufacture shots intentionally, but you will also learn to pinpoint your faults simply by looking at the flight of the ball as it curves through the air.

TECHNIQUE

THE DRAW SHOT

The draw shot (sometimes known as the hook) is when you impart sufficient spin to the ball for it to swing to the left once it is in the air. Shown here is an ideal situation in which to play the draw. With water on the left of the fairway, you can aim down the right and let the ball drift back towards the middle.

3 ◀ In the backswing, concentrate on making a good turn, swinging in a rounded action as opposed to keeping a straight back.

1 ◀ Aim the clubface at the target, then align your feet, hips and shoulders slightly to the right of that. How far right you aim depends on how much draw-spin you require. Note that the spin makes the ball run further than normal, so allow for this when you consider club selection and a landing area.

4 ◀ At the top of the backswing, the shaft of the club should point to the right of the target. How far right depends on how far you intend to shape the ball.

2 ◀ Strengthen your left-hand grip just a fraction by twisting it anti-clockwise slightly so that three or three-and-a-half knuckles show from the front instead of the normal two. This helps keep the clubface closed in your stance and further encourages a draw. Note that the club should still be pointing at the target.

5 ◀ As you swing down, attack the ball from "inside" the line, sweeping the club across the target line from left to right. The clubface is not closed to the target, it is aiming straight at it, but in relation to your stance and the path of your swing, it is closed. This will impart the side-spin to the ball to make it move from right to left through the air.

TECHNIQUE
THE LOW FADE

The fade (or slice in its extreme form), is the opposite of the draw and hook. Therefore, you need to create the exact opposite impact factors in order to make the ball spin the other way. Here, a tree is blocking a direct path to the hole — and it is too close to fire straight over it. A low, cutting fade is the best shot to use.

2 ▼ Choke down on the grip a few centimetres (an inch or two) and weaken your left-hand hold by moving it slightly clockwise. This helps ensure that the clubface does not close to the left at impact.

1 ◀ Aim the clubface at the target, but this time align your hips, feet and shoulders to the left of the line. This encourages you to swing very slightly from out-to-in, which helps impart the necessary side-spin.

3 ◀ Swing back along the line of your feet for the first 45 cm (18 in) of the takeaway. Try to make your swing a little more upright than normal.

4 At the top of the back-swing, the shaft of the club should point to the left of the target. Ask a friend to check this for you, or practise it at home in front of a mirror.

6 Note how the follow-through is slightly "held-off". That is a positive sign for this type of shot. The angles you create at address ensure that the clubhead travels slightly across the line, or out-to-in, through impact. As the clubface is open in relation to the path of your swing, you automatically create the necessary side-spin to produce a shot that starts to the left, then fades to the right through the air.

5 In the down-swing the clubhead approaches the ball from out-side the target line. Again, geometry does the hard work for you. Through impact, try to sense that the back of your left hand faces the target for just a fraction longer than normal. This ensures that you maintain the necessary clubface angle to create side-spin on the ball.

TECHNIQUE
THE HIGH SHOT OVER THE TOP

Here the same tree is blocking a path towards the hole. If you doubt your chances of playing the big left-to-right shot, there is an alternative — hoist the ball straight over the top. This is not as risky as it sounds, provided you have a good, solid understanding of the necessary techniques.

As we have already seen, working the ball in different ways through the air is a game of opposites. When you need to lift the ball high into the air, you should merely think of adopting the opposite techniques from those required to hit the ball low.

1 ◄ Settle more of your weight on the right side than on the left; a ratio of roughly 60/40 is perfect. The ball should be 5 to 8 cm (2 to 3 in) further forward in your stance. This helps position your upper body in behind the ball and automatically places your hands directly above the clubhead, which will cause a little more loft than on a conventional shot.

2 ◄ This is the position shown in step 1, seen from the front. Note the hands are directly above the clubhead.

3 ◄ Swing the club back a little more steeply than normal to try to encourage the necessary steep angle of attack in the downswing.

4 ◀ Above all, try to stay behind the ball as much as possible through the hitting area.

5 ◀ Keep your head hanging back behind the point of impact, until the momentum of your arms and the clubhead pull you through.

6 ◀ All you then need to do is finish high, in perfect balance, and watch the ball soar over the tree-top.

TECHNIQUE
SLOPING LIES

The way to play a good shot from an uphill or downhill lie is to alter your set-up in such a way that you can swing normally.

THE UPHILL LIE

First, take a look at the uphill lie. Straight away you should recognize that the upslope will make the ball fly much higher than normal, so take a longer club than you would on a flat lie from the same distance. You will also have a tendency to pull the shot left, so allow for this when you aim.

THE DOWNHILL LIE

From the downhill lie, you must use a shorter club than usual to gain any loft on your shot. Again, the key is to build your stance around the slope.

THE UPHILL LIE

1 ◄ At address, position the ball a fraction further forward and try to set your shoulders on a fairly level plane with the slope of the fairway. You will find that your head is well behind the ball, and you should endeavour to maintain that relationship at least until impact. Your stance is now as normal as it can possibly be – you have built your position around the slope.

2 ◄ Transferring your weight in the backswing should not be a problem – the slope is helping you in that regard – so make sure that at the top of the backswing your body weight is supported over a flexed right knee.

3 ◄ In the downswing, just concentrate on swinging the clubhead along the contours of the slope, through impact, to a balanced finish.

THE DOWNHILL LIE

1 ◄ With the ball back in your stance, set your shoulders as level to the slope as you can comfortably manage. You should also keep your weight fractionally over the left side – a ratio of 60/40 is ideal.

2 ◄ Your main thought in the backswing should be to make a good turn. The down-slope will naturally keep your weight more centred over the ball. You need to make sure that your weight does not shift further down the slope.

3 ▲ In the downswing you must resist the tendency to help the ball into the air – that will only lead to a poor strike. Accept the fact that the ball will fly lower than normal and commit yourself to swinging the clubhead as far down the slope as possible – almost as if you are chasing after the ball as it flies. Practise this technique with a number of clubs – for example, your 9-iron, pitching-wedge and sand-wedge. This will enable you to use exactly the same swing without any conscious manipulation, while varying the distance you can hit the ball.

EXERCISE
VARY YOUR PRACTICE

1 ◄ On the practice ground, select a mid-iron and "call the shots". Hit a fade with one ball and a draw with the next, then a high shot followed by a low shot. Learn how to get from A to B in several ways. In this position, with the ball below the level of your feet, you are forced to bend over a little more from the hips.

3 ◄ Conversely, when the ball is above your feet it is necessary to stand a little more upright.

2 ◄ This alters your spine angle and leads to a more upright swing plane. That tends to result in a shot that fades to the right.

4 ◄ This leads to a more rounded swing plane, which tends to cause you to draw the ball. Learning to allow for these deviations makes you better equipped to handle sloping lies on the course. Practising a variety of shots also makes you aware of the position of the clubhead throughout the swing – and that is very good for your golf. Sloping lies affect the flight of the ball through the air, so practise from these situations too.

STRATEGY

Smart strategy is the inconspicuous element of good golf. It doesn't manifest itself in spectacular fashion, like a towering long drive; nor does it turn heads and cause gasps. But your strategic ability, or course management as it is often referred to, is at least as important as anything else you do in the space of 18 holes. Tom Watson is recognized as one of the great thinkers of the game. His extraordinary record is due in no small part to his immense powers of thinking and strategic shot-making. So if you want to shoot the best possible score, then it is time to get a smarter strategy.

TECHNIQUE
KNOW YOUR DISTANCES

The first step towards good course management skills is to learn precisely how far you hit using every club in your bag. Even though you may not strike the ball with a high level of consistency, you should be able to determine an average for each club. That enables you to make positive judgements on the course, rather than having to rely on guesswork and the vagaries of luck.

FIND YOUR AVERAGE

Go to the practice ground with a full set of clubs and a bucket of balls and carry out the following exercise. Using whichever club you like best, hit 20 balls. Then discard the longest five and the shortest five. Pace out the measurements of the main cluster of balls to arrive at the average distance you hit that particular club. Write the information down on a notepad, and repeat the exercise with every club in your bag.

It takes time, but this exercise is worth every minute you invest. Even if you play the same course week in, week out — in fact, especially if you play the same course — knowing how far you hit each club gives you the confidence to swing freely. And that means more accurate iron shots.

▶ Getting to know the distances between holes on your local course will enable you to plan your shots better.

EXERCISE
TEE UP INTELLIGENTLY

1 ◄ If you have a natural tendency to hit the ball left-to-right, like most golfers, you should tee your ball on the extreme right of the teeing ground, and aim at the left side of the fairway. Aim at the fat part of the fairway, which is particularly significant when there is trouble, such as a clutch of bunkers, on the right-hand side. If you fade your ball, as planned, the ball finishes in the middle of the fairway – perfect. If you hit the shot dead-straight, you finish in the left half of the fair-way, or at worst, the light rough. If your fade turns into a slice, there is still a good chance that you will find the fairway, or perhaps the light rough on the right. Your target area is increased enormously.

2 ► This is a tough par-3, played over water to a green that angles away from you. Teeing up on the left side of the teeing ground will make it more difficult. Even if you aim at the middle of the green, your margin for error is slender. And if you go for the pin, you will effectively give yourself more water to fly over.

3 ► Look what happens when you tee up on the right side. From there you can aim more easily at the middle of the green, thus introducing a greater margin for error on either side. There is even a better angle from which to attain the pin, situated where it is on the back right edge. On daunting holes such as this, every little helps.

ETIQUETTE

Etiquette in golf means more than just a handshake. The term encompasses a whole set of principles for showing consideration to your fellow players and to the course. Failure to observe these codes of conduct is one of the most common pitfalls for the beginner, so you should be aware of a few simple rules from the first moment you step on to a course.

CARE OF THE COURSE

Failure to repair damage to the golf course during a round is unforgivable. If you have ever experienced the frustration of having to play from a footmark in a bunker or from a divot in the fairway, you will probably have stronger words of your own to describe those who fail to look after the course.

FOOTPRINTS IN THE SAND

◀ One of the most annoying mistakes is when someone leaves footprints and club marks behind in a sand bunker. Before exiting a bunker, always smooth the marks you have made with the rake provided. Do not just walk straight up the face of the bunker and continue to play on. If there is no rake, try to use your club as best you can. The ideal is to leave the bunker in the same state in which you would wish to find it.

REPAIR YOUR PITCH MARKS

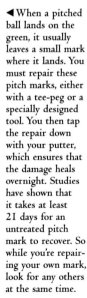

◀When a pitched ball lands on the green, it usually leaves a small mark where it lands. You must repair these pitch marks, either with a tee-peg or a specially designed tool. You then tap the repair down with your putter, which ensures that the damage heals overnight. Studies have shown that it takes at least 21 days for an untreated pitch mark to recover. So while you're repairing your own mark, look for any others at the same time.

SPIKE MARKS

◀ Spike marks on the line of play cannot be repaired, so you should try to avoid dragging your shoes on the green in such a way that might cause damage.

HOLES IN THE FAIRWAY

1 ◀ It is easy to accidentally lift a divot in the fairway, whether as a result of a practice swing or proper shot. Don't panic – all golfers have done it at some stage.

2 ▲ You should always take the time to retrieve the divot and replace it in the hole you have created.

3 ▼ Tread it down securely. In time, the grass will naturally repair itself. This treatment isn't necessary in the rough.

COURTESY AND COMMON SENSE

Golf is a social game, where you normally play a round with other people, whether as opponents or simply as playing partners. They are entitled to play without any hindrance or irritation caused by thoughtlessness on your part. A few simple actions can help ensure that others enjoy their golf as much as you do.

SLOW PLAY

One of the biggest problems in club golf, and one that can quickly bring down the wrath of other players on the beginner, is that of slow play. While you don't want to rush your shot, there are a few steps you can take to speed up your progress around the course.

While your partner is playing their shot, don't just stand there and idly watch. Instead you should be thinking about and preparing for your own shot, so you can play immediately afterwards. After a tee shot, try to walk from the tee directly to your ball — not via your playing partner's ball. Once at the green, another tip is to leave your golf bag on the same side as the next tee — then you can collect it on your way.

LOST BALLS

If your ball goes into rough and is well hidden, you should ask any players behind to play through. Don't waste time searching — wave them through immediately. It's easier in the long run and prevents delays and frayed tempers on the tee behind. Don't be ashamed — even top players lose balls occasionally.

PLACE THE PIN

1 ▲ When you are playing on the green, always place the flag down gently. Don't throw or drop it. You can easily damage the pitch if you are careless with the flag pole.

2 ▲ It doesn't take much abuse for a carefully prepared putting surface to show severe signs of wear and tear. Lack of care on the green will irritate your fellow golfers and it is expensive for the club to maintain the green to a high standard.

THE PLACE TO BE

1 ◄ Golf is hard enough without distractions, so when someone is playing a stroke, stand behind them and slightly to the right, out of their eye-line.

2 ► If the player is left-handed, you need to stand slightly to their left instead. But whatever way they swing, don't stand directly behind your partner.

3 ◄ You need to think of safety as well as courtesy, by making sure you are not standing too close when your partner is taking his shot.

INDEX

The publishers would like to
thank Johanna Head for the
photographs demonstrating
perfect posture, and Mizuno
for the photographs of golf
equipment on pages 10-11.

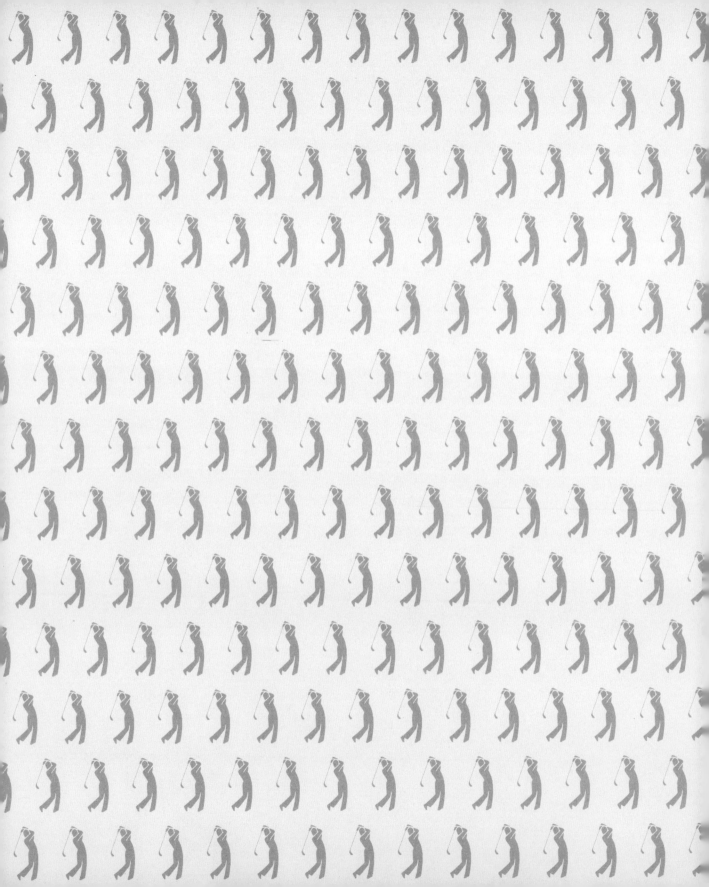